50 *Great ways with* MINCE

50 *Great ways with* MINCE

MAKING THE MOST OF GROUND MEAT IN 50 FANTASTIC RECIPES AND 300 PHOTOGRAPHS

 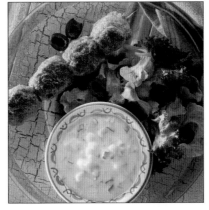 

JENNY STACEY

LORENZ BOOKS

For my husband Steve, and mother Joy, with much love and thanks

This edition is published by Lorenz Books, an imprint of Anness Publishing Ltd, Blaby Road, Wigston, Leicestershire LE18 4SE; info@anness.com

www.lorenzbooks.com; www.annesspublishing.com

If you like the images in this book and would like to investigate using them for publishing, promotions or advertising, please visit our website www.practicalpictures.com for more information.

© Anness Publishing Ltd 2013

Publisher: Joanna Lorenz
Editors: Joanne Rippin, Anne Hildyard
Photographer: James Duncan
Home Economist: Elizabeth Silver

For all recipes, quantities are given in both metric and imperial measures, and where appropriate, measures are also given in standard cups and spoons. Follow one set, but not a mixture, because they are not interchangeable.

PUBLISHER'S NOTE
Although the advice and information in this book are believed to be accurate and true at the time of going to press, neither the authors nor the publisher can accept any legal responsibility or liability for any errors or omissions that may have been made nor for any inaccuracies nor for any loss, harm or injury that comes about from following instructions or advice in this book.

Contents

Introduction

Minced beef has long been a part of our diet, but a wider variety of prepared minced meats, such as turkey, chicken, pork and lamb, is also readily available in supermarkets and butchers. They can be used in a vast range of both simple and more unusual recipes to cook at home.

Mince may be used both for the traditional recipes which we have come to know and love, or in more exotic foreign recipes, and in quick and easy dishes when time is of the essence. Full of protein, mince can make a nutritional meal

Below: Chicken bouche is a puff pastry case with an appetizing filling of minced chicken, mushrooms and redcurrants.

when it is used in pies, rissoles, casseroles, bakes and sauces, and served with potatoes, rice or pasta and a variety of seasonal vegetables.

Whenever possible, extra-lean minced lamb and beef should be purchased as these contain less fat and are of a higher quality, which results in a better and much healthier end product. Turkey mince is a good alternative since it is low in fat, calories and cholesterol. it is perfect for any dish that requires minced meat, for example turkey bolognese or turkey burgers. Pork mince contains more fat but it is flavourful when used in recipes such as chow mein.

Mince is an excellent basic foodstuff to which many different flavourings may be added, making it stretch a little further for more economical cooking. Traditionally used for burgers and chilli con carne, mince has many other inventive uses. It may be served in pies, rissoles, popovers, as a filling for jacket potatoes, or as a stuffing for naan or calzone, all perfect for filling and nutritious family meals.

If you have a mincing machine or food processor, fish, shellfish and other meats not commercially sold as mince may be put through the machine and used in imaginative ways to create wonderful and innovative recipes. When using this book you really will become aware of the versatility of mince, and its endless potential as a base for many creative and flavoursome dishes.

Right: Minced beef makes a flavourful Italian sauce to serve with pasta, as in Spaghetti Bolognese.

Equipment

When using mince, a minimum of basic equipment is required, with items found in the majority of kitchens.

Casserole dish
A covered casserole dish is a must to produce some of the dishes in the book. The lid not only seals in flavour, but prevents food from drying out while cooking.

Chopping boards
Nylon chopping boards are recommended for use as they do not hold flavours and are more hygienic. They must be disinfected so that the cuts do not harbour germs.

Colanders
Used for draining large quantities of food.

Cutters
For stamping out shapes and for making croûtes.

Garlic press
The quickest way to crush garlic to add to mince recipes.

Grater
For grating cheeses and vegetables for addition to the recipes.

Knives
A set of good cooking knives is essential for chopping meat and vegetables to add to the recipes.

Loaf tin
Used to make meatloaf, this tin is easy to use as it has collapsible sides, making turning out easy.

Grinder
Used to grind raw or cooked meat for use in hamburger recipes, providing the correct textured meat.

Mixing bowls
A variety of different sizes are useful for mixing ingredients.

Party brush
For brushing and glazing pastry with beaten egg, and oiling and greasing baking trays and dishes.

Patty tins
Used for popovers, these individual sized tins are ideal for producing small portions for children.

Spoons
Essential to cooking, these spoons do not absorb tastes or germs, so making them more hygienic than wooden spoons. They are also heat-resistant.

Thermometer
Essential for checking the correct cooking temperatures when deep-frying ingredients for hamburger recipes without using a deep-fat fryer.

From top left: colander; sieves; loaf tin; casserole dish; mixing bowls; thermometer; grater; on the patty tins – knives; pastry brush; spoon; on the white chopping board – cutters; mincer; garlic press, and salt and pepper mills.

Herbs

Herbs, both dried and fresh, can be used to enhance the taste of mince dishes. Certain herbs have an affinity with specific foods, for example, dill and fish, and basil and tomatoes.

Basil
There are several types of basil, varying in shades and taste. Basil and tomatoes is a classic combination used for spaghetti sauces, soups, stews and rice dishes.

Chives
Rich in vitamins A and C and a member of the onion family, chives are added to enhance the taste, although long cooking reduces this. Mainly used in salads, soups and sauces, this herb adds taste and is used for simple presentation.

Dill
Both the seeds and leaves are very useful for cooking. Each have a distinctive taste. The leaves are added to soft cheeses, seafood, salads and meat sauces.

Oregano
Has a close affinity with marjoram, but marjoram has a more delicate aroma. Used for pizzas, salad dressings, in Greek dishes and many other ground meat dishes. Excellent in tomato sauces, fresh marjoram and oregano have a better taste than the dried variety.

Parsley
Both curly and flat leaf parsley are rich in vitamins and minerals. Used in omelettes, for garnishes, soups, vegetable dishes, mixed with soft cheeses, eggs, sauces and with ground meat.

Rosemary
An aromatic herb with a pungent strong aroma. Excellent in jams and jellies and particularly good with lamb and other meats.

Tarragon
Has a subtle aniseed taste. French tarragon is often used mixed with soft cheeses, sauces, chicken dishes, in dressings, poultry, egg dishes and with fish. Along with parsley, chives and chervil, it is one of the four *fines herbes*.

Thyme
Over 100 species of thyme exist. Thyme blends well with most ingredients and other herbs and is used extensively in meat stews. Delicious with sauteed and baked vegetables, it is also added to enhance stuffings that are used for roast meats.

Below: Oregano

Left: Rosemary

Right: Parsley

Below: Tarragon

Below: Basil   *Right: Chives*

Right: Dill

Left: Thyme

Spices

Dried spices are essential ingredients in cooking. Used in small quantities they should be stored in airtight containers to prevent loss of aroma and strength of taste.

Chillies

Originating from Mexico, there are many varieties available, such as dried, red, green and yellow. Chillies are a member of the pepper family and have a sweet, fiery and hot taste. They are used around the world in many spicy dishes containing hamburger or other ground meats. The seeds are hot and may be removed before cooking. Excellent in tomato sauces with meat, beans and lentils. Ground chilli powder is a blend of chillies and spices.

Coriander

Available both fresh and dried. It is native to the Middle East and has a strong distinctive scent. The leaves have a slightly aniseed taste but the seeds are sweeter. Extensively used in curries and spicy dishes, soups and stews.

Cumin

An Eastern spice with a warm distinctive aroma. Very valuable in Indian, Eastern and Mediterranean dishes. Excellent with couscous, curries and stews.

Garam masala

An Indian spice mix of cumin, coriander seeds, cardamom, pepper, cloves and cinnamon. Used extensively in curries and spicy meat dishes.

Ground ginger

Has a fresh spicy, lemony aroma and is used extensively in oriental cooking, curries and meat dishes.

Above from top left: ground cumin, garam masala, saffron, turmeric, chilli, ginger, paprika, coriander and mixed peppercorns.

Mixed peppercorns

Often sold as a mixture, these green, black, white and red dried berries of the pepper vine produce a hot mixture which when ground into dishes, brings out and enhances tastes.

Paprika

This spice is the ground powder of dried, ripe sweet peppers. A mixture of mild and hot peppers are used and the spice adds a tangy warmth to meat and vegetable dishes, as well as producing a powder that is a lovely earthy shade of red.

Saffron

Made from the stigmas of a crocus, saffron adds a yellow shade and a nutty taste. The threads are superior to ground saffron. Used with fish, poultry and beef.

Turmeric

An Indian spice that can be used as a substitute for saffron, but for appearance, not taste. Adds a mild aroma to foods.

Store Cupboard

Minced meats are perfect partners for many common store cupboard ingredients to produce quick, tasty meals and snacks, from classic western dishes to international favourites.

Barbecue sauce
Thick in texture and made from fruit, sugar, chilli and vinegar, it is brown with a sharp, acidic taste.

Breadcrumbs
Can be used both fresh and dried. May be added as a bulking agent in hamburger dishes and used for coating purposes, such as rissoles, or for a crispy top on a bake.

Bulgur wheat or cracked wheat
May be used in hamburger recipes. Processed from semolina.

Chickpeas
Both whole and split, they may be used in casseroles, stuffings and soups. They are available canned or dried, and are used in Middle Eastern recipes.

Chilli sauce
Can be mild or very spicy. Made from tomatoes, peppers and spices, it is added to many mince recipes.

Cranberry sauce
A condiment traditionally served with turkey, made from cranberries, sugar and vinegar. Excellent for poultry recipes.

Dried apricots
The 'no-need-to-soak' variety can be eaten and used from the packet. Excellent with ground lamb in a classic tagine, they add an authentic fruitiness, and enhance the taste of the meat.

Horseradish
The grated root of the horseradish plant, it has a fieriness that traditionally complements beef dishes. Made with vinegar and cream it is also good with robust fish such as mackerel.

Kidney beans
Used extensively in Mexican cooking and complement many hamburger dishes. They are available canned or dried.

Mayonnaise
An emulsion of eggs, oil and lemon. Used in many cold dishes and as a dip.

Mustard
There are many types of mustard available, in both the powdered form and ready made. Each are blends of different mustard seeds, mixed with vinegar and herbs to give a wide range of tastes and degrees of hotness, the stronger ones being most suitable with milder foods.

Oatmeal
Rolled oats are ground to varying degrees, either coarse or fine. They are often used as a bulking agent in cooking, or to make a crispy coating or topping.

Rice
Used to thicken soups or casseroles, or as an accompaniment to mop up a sauce. There are many types: long grain is used frequently, mixed with wild rice for a more special dish.

Sesame seeds
With the highest oil content of any seed, the seeds and oil are used widely in oriental cooking, owing to their very distinctive strong nutty aroma. The taste of sesame seeds can be enhanced by dry roasting and then adding to rice, fish, meat and vegetable dishes.

Soy sauce
A dark salty sauce, made by fermenting soya beans and roasted barley and wheat. There are many varieties of the sauce, ranging from light, which is thin and salty, to dark, which is richer in taste and shade and is thicker than the light version. Some types feature a lower salt content. Soy sauce is used extensively in Chinese and Japanese cooking, and it enhances meat dishes, soups and stews.

Spring roll sauce
A commercially available Chinese sauce, made from tomatoes, chillies and spices. Served with many Chinese recipes or as a dip for spring rolls and dumplings.

Right: Some useful ingredients that you can keep in the store cupboard. The selection includes three types of rice, oatmeal, bulgur wheat, dried apricots, chickpeas and kidney beans, mustard, sesame seeds, soy sauce, mayonnaise, chilli sauce, barbecue sauce, tomato ketchup, horseradish sauce, spring roll sauce, cranberry sauce and breadcrumbs.

Fresh Ingredients

Many fresh ingredients complement minced beef, other meats and fish, adding flavour, colour and texture to create a vast range of bakes, casseroles, pastries and pizzas.

Aubergine
A native to India, the purple aubergine is the most common. It is eaten cooked and is used in classic mince dishes.

Cheddar cheese
Made from cows' milk, available in mild and mature flavours. Good for sauces, and grated to melt on toppings.

Chilli peppers
May be sweet or hot in a variety of colours and sizes. The sweet pepper has a milder flavour and may be eaten raw.

Gruyere cheese
From Swiss cows' milk. Excellent for melting. It adds a nutty taste to sauces and can be used as a topping.

Mozzarella cheese
An unripened curd cheese with a mild creamy flavour. It melts well and is very suitable for use on pizzas.

Onion
Spanish onions are large and mild and used extensively in cooking. Red onions are milder, with a sweet flavour.

Parmesan cheese
An Italian cheese which is used for grating in cooking. Excellent in sauces. It can add flavour to dried mixtures.

Rice
A form of carbohydrate, it is used to serve with mince dishes such as chilli con carne and stroganoff.

Sausages
Can be herby or spicy. All kinds add flavour to mince dishes and help to extend the mince a little further.

Sour cream
A savoury cream, soured with lemon juice. Used as a topping and in dips.

Spinach
May be used raw in salads or blanched and cooked in dishes. Adds flavour and colour to many mince dishes.

Spring onions
Very colourful and mild in taste. Used raw in salads and Chinese cooking to add colour and flavour.

Tomatoes
Available all the year round in varying shapes and sizes. They can be stuffed, sliced for salads or cooked in sauces with mince, and used for garnishes.

Left: A variety of the fresh ingredients that complement minced meats.

Basic Sauté

This cooking method forms the basis of many mince recipes. Meat is cooked in a small amount of oil to tenderize and seal in the flavours, before adding liquid and any other ingredients.

1 Heat a little oil in a large, heavy frying pan for I minute.

2 Add the minced meat and sauté gently for 7 minutes, stirring to prevent sticking.

3 Continue cooking the meat until it is browned and sealed.

Dry-frying

An alternative to the basic saute, dry frying is a healthier way to seal meats as it does not require any additional fat or oil. Choose a non-stick saucepan and do not turn up the heat too high, or the meat may stick.

1 Heat a non-stick coated frying pan gently over a low flame.

2 Add the minced meat, breaking up any lumps with a heatproof spoon.

3 Sauté for 5 minutes, stirring until the meat is browned and sealed.

Stir-frying

An increasingly popular cooking method, which it is healthier because it uses less fat. Foods are quickly fried in a hot wok or heavy-based frying pan with a small amount of oil.

1 Heat a wok over a low flame.

2 Add the oil and heat it until it is almost smoking.

3 Add the ingredients and fry over a high heat, stirring constantly until the meat is browned and cooked through.

Blanching

This tenderizes foods, cooking them slightly before further use. An ideal way to loosen the skin of ingredients such as tomatoes and nuts, making them easier to peel.

1 Trim the top from the tomatoes and, using a spoon, scoop out the central flesh and seeds.

2 Bring a large saucepan of water to the boil, add the tomatoes and blanch for about 5 minutes.

3 Remove the tomatoes with a draining spoon, refresh in cold water, and upturn onto a piece of absorbent kitchen paper.

Mincing – with a Food Processor

Foods such as fish and prawns are ideal for mincing in a food processor, using the chopping blade. A quick method of producing a basic mince for recipes.

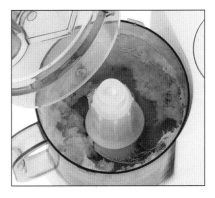

1 Wash the fish and remove the skin and any small bones.

2 Flake the fish and place in a food processor fitted with a chopping blade.

3 Process the fish for 30 seconds on high speed or until finely minced.

Mincing – with a Mincer

This is the traditional piece of equipment used to mince both cooked and raw ingredients. Blades of several different sizes come with a mincer, allowing different textured mince to be produced.

1 Trim excess fat from the meat and chop the meat into small pieces. Attach the mincer to a work surface and place a bowl underneath. Select the required blade.

2 Feed the meat into the top of the mincer, turning the handle all the time. Use the minced meat as required.

Quick Barbecue Relish

Making use of storecupboard ingredients, this fast and easy relish takes only minutes to make and is ideal to serve with burgers, patties and other quick recipes. It has a slightly tangy flavour.

Ingredients
45 ml/3 tbsp sweet pickle
15 ml/1 tbsp Worcestershire sauce
30 ml/2 tbsp tomato ketchup
10 ml/2 tsp prepared mustard
15 ml/1 tbsp cider vinegar
30 ml/2 tbsp brown sauce

1 Spoon the sweet pickle in to a bowl.

COOK'S TIP
All these relishes should be used as quickly as possible, but will keep, covered, for up to a week in the refrigerator.

2 Stir in the Worcestershire sauce, tomato ketchup and prepared mustard.

3 Add the vinegar and brown sauce and mix well. Chill and use as required.

Tomato Relish

A cooked relish which may be served hot or cold. It has a concentrated tomato flavour, making it ideal to serve with pasta, rissoles, burgers, rice and many of the snack recipes in the book.

Ingredients
15 ml/1 tbsp olive oil
1 onion, chopped
1 garlic clove, crushed
25 g/1 oz/2 tbsp flour
30 ml/2 tbsp tomato ketchup
300 ml/1/2 pint/11/4 cups passata
5 ml/1 tsp sugar
15 ml/1 tbsp chopped fresh parsley

1 Heat the oil in a pan. Add the onion and garlic clove and sauté for 5 minutes.

2 Add the flour, stir in to the onion mixture and cook for I minute.

3 Stir in the tomato ketchup, passata, sugar and fresh parsley. Bring to the boil. Chill and use as required.

Chilli Relish

Not for the faint hearted, this fiery relish is ideal to serve with savoury snacks such as pies, burgers or rissoles. For a slightly milder flavour, remove the seeds from the chilli before using.

Ingredients

2 large tomatoes
1 red onion
10 ml/2 tsp chilli sauce
15 ml/l tbsp chopped fresh basil
1 green chilli, chopped
pinch of salt
pinch of sugar

1 Finely chop the tomatoes and place in a mixing bowl.

2 Finely chop the onion and add to the tomatoes with the chilli sauce.

3 Stir in the fresh basil, chilli, salt and sugar. Use as required.

Cucumber Relish

A cool, refreshing relish, it may also be used as a dip with recipes such as rissoles, or as a topping on burgers and patties. It should be stored for as short a time as possible.

Ingredients

½ cucumber
2 celery sticks, chopped
1 green pepper, seeded and chopped
1 garlic clove, crushed
300 ml/½ pint/1¼ cups natural yogurt
15 ml/1 tbsp chopped fresh coriander
freshly ground black pepper

1 Dice the cucumber and place in a large bowl. Add the celery, green pepper and crushed garlic.

2 Stir in the yogurt and chopped fresh coriander. Season with the pepper. Cover with clear film and chill.

Basic Bolognese Sauce

A simple, basic recipe which can be used as the basis for many more recipes. The sauce gains flavour if made ahead, and is equally good served with pasta, rice or jacket potatoes.

Ingredients
15 ml/1 tbsp olive oil
15 g/½ oz/1 tbsp unsalted butter
1 onion, chopped
2 garlic cloves, crushed
450 g/1 1b/4 cups minced beef
15 g/1 tbsp flour
300 ml/2 tbsp tomato purée
300 ml/½ pint/1¼ cups beef stock
1 x 400 g/14 oz can chopped
tomatoes, with their juice
salt and freshly ground black pepper

1 Heat the oil and butter in a large pan. Add the onion, garlic and minced beef. Cook for 7 minutes until browned.

2 Stir in the flour and cook for a further minute. Add the tomato purée.

3 Stir in the stock and canned tomatoes Season. Use for one of the variations (right), or simmer for 50 minutes.

Chilli Bean Bolognese Sauce

Making use of the basic sauce, this recipe shows the versatility of mince. The addition of a red chilli, chilli powder, beans and corn gives the sauce an spicy, authentic Mexican flavour.

Ingredients
1 x basic recipe Basic Bolognese
    Sauce (above)
1 x 200 g/7 oz can red kidney
    beans, drained
1 x 200 g/7 oz can black-eyed
    beans, drained
1 red chilli, sliced
50 g/2 oz baby sweetcorn, halved
5 ml/1 tsp chilli powder
15 ml/1 tbsp chopped fresh parsley
salt and freshly ground black pepper

1 Make up the Basic Bolognese Sauce. Add the kidney beans and black-eyed beans, then stir in the red chilli.

2 Add the chilli powder, then stir in the sweetcorn and cook over a low heat for 50 minutes.

3 Stir in the chopped fresh parsley. Season and use as required.

Vegetable Bolognese Sauce

For those who like a little crunch in their meals, this dish is ideal. The vegetables add colour and flavour to the basic sauce, making a suitable filling for lasagne or cannelloni.

Ingredients

1 x basic recipe Basic Bolognese
    Sauce (opposite)
1 carrot
2 celery stalks
1 courgette
1 green pepper
25 g/1 oz/⅓ cup sun-dried tomatoes
50 g/2 oz small broccoli florets

1 Make up the Basic Bolognese Sauce from the recipe opposite. Dice the carrot and add to the sauce.

2 Chop the celery stalks and courgette and stir into the sauce.

3 Seed and dice the green pepper and chop the sun-dried tomatoes. Add to the sauce with the broccoli florets. Stir well and cook for 50 minutes. Use as required.

Mushroom and Bacon Bolognese Sauce

This sauce has a lovely smoky flavour, which is absorbed by the mushrooms. It is a delicious sauce to serve with rice, or it can be used as the basis for a casserole or minced beef pie.

Ingredients

1 x basic recipe Basic Bolognese Sauce
    (opposite)
4 rashers bacon
50 g/2 oz smoked sausage
2 large open cap mushrooms
15 ml/1 tbsp chopped fresh oregano

1 Make up the Basic Bolognese Sauce. Remove the bacon rind and cut the bacon into strips. Stir into the sauce.

2 Slice the sausage, add to the sauce, mix together then cook on a low heat for about 40 minutes.

3 Peel and slice the mushrooms and add to the sauce with the fresh oregano. Cook for a further 10 minutes. Use as required.

Dim Sum

Traditionally served in the afternoon with tea, dim sum is a style of Chinese food, usually served in bite-size portions as steamed or deep-fried dumplings.

Serves 4

For the dough
150 g/5 oz/1¼ cups plain flour
50 ml/2 fl oz/¼ cup boiling water
25 ml/1 fl oz/⅛ cup cold water
7.5 m/½ tbsp vegetable oil

For the filling
75 g/3 oz/¾ cup minced pork
45 ml/3 tbsp chopped canned
 bamboo shoots
7.5 m/½ tbsp light soy sauce
5 ml/1 tsp dry sherry
5 ml/1 tsp demerara sugar
2.5 m/½ tsp sesame oil
5 ml/1 tsp cornflour
lettuce leaves such as iceberg, frisée
 or Webb lettuce

1 For the dough, sift the flour into a bowl. Stir in the boiling water, then the cold water together with the oil. Mix to form a dough and knead until smooth.

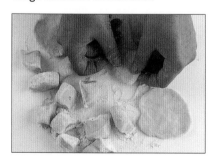

2 Divide the mixture into sixteen equal pieces and shape into circles.

3 For the filling, mix together the pork, bamboo shoots, soy sauce, sherry, sugar and oil.

4 Stir in the cornflour.

5 Place a little of the filling in the centre of each dim sum circle. Use your finger and thumb to pinch the edges of the dough together to form little "purses".

6 Line a steamer with a damp dish towel. Place the dim sum in the steamer and steam for 5-10 minutes. Serve on a bed of lettuce with soy sauce, spring onion curls, sliced red chilli and prawn crackers.

VARIATION
Substitute the pork with peeled prawns. Sprinkle 15ml/1 tbsp of sesame seeds on to the dim sum before steaming.

Beef Chilli Soup

A hearty dish based on a traditional chilli recipe, this soup is ideal to serve with fresh crusty bread as a warming start to any meal.

Serves 4

15 ml/1 tbsp oil
1 onion, chopped
175 g/6 oz/1½ cups minced beef
2 garlic cloves, chopped
1 red chilli, sliced
25 g/1 oz/2 tbsp plain flour
1 x 400 g/14 oz can chopped
    tomatoes
600 ml/1 pint/2½ cups beef stock
222 g/8 oz/2 cups canned kidney
    beans, drained
30 ml/2 tbsp chopped fresh parsley
salt and freshly ground black pepper

1 Heat the oil in a large saucepan. Fry the onion and minced beef for 5 minutes until browned and sealed.

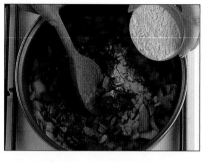

2 Add the garlic, chilli and flour. Cook for l minute. Add the tomatoes and pour in the stock. Bring to the boil.

3 Stir in the kidney beans and season well. Cook for 20 minutes.

4 Add the fresh parsley and season to taste. Serve with crusty bread.

COOK'S TIP
For a milder flavour, remove the seeds from the chilli after slicing.

Samosas

A variation on a popular Indian starter, these golden samosas have a spicy meat and vegetable filling. Delicious served with traditional accompaniments or just as a snack.

Serves 4

15 ml/1 tbsp oil
115 g/4 oz/1 cup minced beef
3 spring onions, sliced
50 g/2 oz baby sweetcorn, chopped
I carrot, diced
2.5 m1/½ tsp ground cumin
2.5 m1/½ tsp ground coriander
5 ml/1tsp curry paste
2 fl oz/50 ml/¼ cup beef stock
6 sheets filo pastry
25 g/1 oz/2 tbsp melted butter
oil for deep-frying
fresh coriander to garnish
lime pickle and poppadums,
    to serve

1 Heat the oil in a frying pan. Fry the minced beef for 5 minutes until browned and sealed.

2 Add the spring onions, sweetcorn, carrot, cumin, coriander and the curry paste. Cook for a further 5 minutes. Add the beef stock and bring the mixture to the boil.

3 Cut each filo sheet into eight. Brush one sheet with melted butter, place another on top. Brush with butter and repeat to make eight stacks of pastry. Put one-eighth of the filling in the centre of each sheet, brush the edges with butter. Fold into a triangle. Brush with butter.

4 Heat the oil for deep-frying in a large heavy-based pan to I80°C/350°F. Cook the samosas for 5 minutes until golden brown. Drain well and garnish with fresh coriander. Serve with pieces of lime pickle and poppadums.

Spring Rolls

Traditionally a Chinese side dish, these lightly fried spring rolls are popular with everyone. They are good served with spring roll sauce and make a delicious appetizer.

Serves 4

For the filling
15 ml/1 tbsp oil
75 g/3 oz/¾ cup minced beef
15 g/½ oz/1 tbsp plain flour
1 small red pepper, seeded and chopped
1 small green pepper, seeded and chopped
100 g/4 oz beansprouts
5 ml/1 tsp Chinese five-spice powder
15 ml/1 tbsp light soy sauce
50 g/2 oz button mushrooms, chopped

For the spring roll skins
75 g/3 oz/¾ cup plain flour
25 g/l oz/2 tbsp cornflour
30 ml/2 tbsp vegetable oil
300 ml/½ pint/1¼ cups water
oil for deep-frying
spring onion curls, to garnish

1 For the filling, heat the oil in a frying pan. Add the minced beef and fry for 3 minutes until browned and sealed.

2 Add the flour, red and green peppers, beansprouts, Chinese five-spice powder, soy sauce and mushrooms. Cook for a further 5 minutes.

3 For the pancakes, mix together the flour and cornflour. Gradually stir in the oil and water to make a smooth batter.

4 Heat a lightly-oiled l5 cm/6 in omelette pan. Cook one-eighth of the mixture for 2-3 minutes until cooked through. Repeat with the remaining batter, covering the pancakes with a damp dish towel.

5 Place one-eighth of the filling in the centre of each pancake, fold in the ends to encase and roll up.

6 Heat the oil for deep-frying in a large heavy-based pan to 180°C/350°F. Fry the spring rolls one at a time, for 4-5 minutes. Drain and repeat with the remaining spring rolls. Garnish with spring onion curls and serve with spring roll sauce and lettuce leaves.

COOK'S TIP
If you are short of time, you could buy ready-made spring roll wrappers, which can be eaten fresh or deep fried.

Dolmades

These dainty vine leaf parcels are very popular in Mediterranean countries, and they are easy to make at home. They are traditionally served as part of a Greek *mezze*.

Serves 4

8 vine leaves

For the filling
15 ml/1 tbsp olive oil
115 g/4 oz/1 cup minced beef
30 ml/2 tbsp pine nuts
1 onion, chopped
15 ml/1 tbsp chopped fresh coriander
5 ml/1 tsp ground cumin
15 ml/1 tbsp tomato purée
salt and freshly ground black pepper

For the tomato sauce
150 ml/¼ pint/⅔ cup passata
150 ml/¼ pint/⅔ cup beefstock
150 ml/2 tsp caster sugar

1 For the filling, heat the oil in a pan. Add the minced beef, pine nuts and onion. Cook for 5 minutes until browned and sealed.

2 Stir in the fresh coriander, cumin and tomato purée. Cook for a further 3 minutes and season well.

3 Lay eight vine leaves shiny side down on a work surface. Place some filling in the centre of each and fold the stalk end over the filling. Roll up the parcel toward the tip of the leaf and place in a greased flameproof casserole dish, seam side down.

4 For the sauce, mix together the passata, stock and sugar and pour over each vine leaf, Cover and cook on a moderate heat for 3-4 minutes. Reduce the heat and cook for a further 30 minutes. Serve with green and red pepper salad.

Cheesy Tartlets

The minced beef in these mouthwatering little tartlets is seasoned with thyme and leeks, and topped with a tangy cheese sauce to whet the appetite.

Serves 4

225 g/8 oz prepared shortcrust pastry

For the filling
7.5 ml/¹/₂ tbsp oil
115 g/4 oz/1 cup minced beef
7.5 ml/¹/₂ tbsp chopped fresh thyme
1 small leek, sliced
salt and freshly ground black pepper
sliced cherry tomatoes, to garnish
fresh parsley, to garnish

For the cheese sauce
15 g/¹/₂ oz/1 tbsp butter
15 g/¹/₂ oz/1 tbsp plain flour
120 ml/4 fl oz/¹/₂ cup milk
25 g/1 oz/¹/₄ cup freshly grated mature
    Cheddar cheese
2.5 ml/¹/₂ tsp mustard

1 Preheat the oven to 190°C/375°F/ Gas 5. Roll out the pastry and line four 7.5 cm/3 in tartlet tins. Bake blind for 15 minutes.

2 Heat the oil and fry the mince, thyme and leek for 10 minutes. Season and drain.

3 For the cheese sauce, melt the butter in a pan. Add the flour and cook for I minute. Stir in the milk and grated cheese. Bring to the boil, stirring constantly. Add the mustard and season well.

4 Spoon the mince mixture into the base of the tartlet cases, top with the cheese sauce and cook for 10-1 5 minutes in the preheated oven. Serve the tartlets with a crisp green salad.

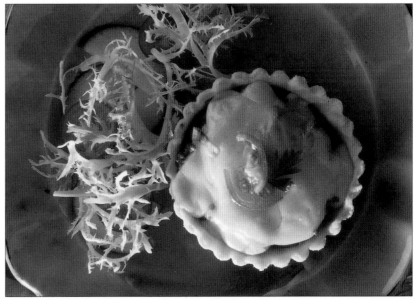

Mexican Tortillas

A variation on a tortilla, this starter, with chilli beef and refried beans, combines all the flavours of Mexico. Served with guacamole and salsa, it is a tasty and colourful dish.

Serves 4

For the tortilia
75 g/2½ oz/½ cup wholemeal flour
10 ml/2 tsp lard
50 ml/2 fl oz/¼ cup water

For the beans
30 ml/2 tbsp oil
450 g/1 lb/4 cups canned borlotti beans
1 onion, chopped
15 ml/1 tbsp chopped fresh coriander

For the filling
175 g/6 oz/1½ cups minced beef
1 onion, chopped
1 red chilli, sliced
2.5 ml/½ tsp chilli powder
2 garlic cloves, chopped
30 ml/2 tbsp tomato purée
soured cream, guacamole and salsa,
    to serve

1 For the tortilla, sift the flour into a bowl. Rub in the lard until the mixture resembles breadcrumbs. Stir in the water to make a soft dough,

2 Knead on a lightly floured surface and cover with a warm, damp towel and leave for I hour. Divide the dough into four. Shape into balls and flatten with a rolling pin. Heat a frying pan flame until hot. Place one portion in the pan and cook for 30 seconds. Turn and cook for a further IO seconds. Cover and keep warm in a low oven. Repeat with the remaining tortillas.

3 Drain the beans then heat the oil in a large pan and fry them together with the onion for I 5 minutes. Mash with a fork and add the fresh coriander. Cook for a further 10 minutes, adding extra oil if necessary.

4 For the filling, dry-fry the minced beef, onion and chilli in a large pan for 3 minutes. Keep stirring all the time.

5 Add the chilli powder, garlic clove and tomato purée. Cook for a further 10 minutes over a low heat.

6 Spoon the beans onto the tortilla and top with the chilli beef mixture. Serve with small bowls of soured cream, guacamole and salsa.

VARIATION
Try canned black beans for a change. Just drain and continue with the recipe in the same way.

Beef Casserole and Dumplings

A classic English recipe, this delicious casserole is topped with light herby dumplings for a warming and nutritious meal, perfect for a cold winter's day.

Serves 4

15 ml/1 tbsp oil
450 g/1 lb/4 cups minced beef
16 button onions
2 carrots, sliced
2 celery sticks, sliced
25 g/1 oz/2 tbsp flour
600 ml/1 pint/2½ cups beef stock
salt and freshly ground black pepper

For the dumplings
115 g/4 oz/1 cup shredded
    vegetable suet
50 g/2 oz/½ cup plain flour
15 ml/1 tbsp chopped fresh parsley
water to mix

1 Preheat the oven to 180°C/350°F/Gas 4. Heat the oil in a flameproof casserole and fry the minced beef for 5 minutes until browned and sealed.

2 Add the onions and fry for 5 minutes, stirring all the time.

3 Stir in the vegetables and flour and cook for a further 1 minute.

4 Add the stock and seasoning. Bring to the boil. Cover and cook in the oven for 1¼ hours.

5 For the dumplings, mix the suet, flour, fresh parsley and water to form a smooth dough.

6 Roll into eight equal-sized balls and place around the top of the casserole for another 20 minutes, uncovered. Serve with broccoli florets.

VARIATION
Any seasonal winter root vegetables can be used for this casserole, and either thyme, rosemary or sage could be used instead of the parsley.

Coconut Curry

Traditional, mild Indian spices with minced beef and fresh coriander make a creamy, flavoursome curry with a hint of coconut.

Serves 4

15 ml/1 tbsp oil
450 g/1 lb/4 cups minced beef
2 garlic cloves, chopped
5 ml/1 tsp ground cumin
5 ml/1 tsp ground coriander
5 ml/1 tsp garam masala
1.25 cm/½ in fresh root ginger, chopped
25 g/1 oz/2 tbsp ground almonds
175 ml/6 fl oz/¾ cup coconut milk
120 ml/4 fl oz/½ cup beef stock
30 ml/2 tbsp chopped fresh coriander
225 g/8 oz/1 cup long grain rice
5 ml/1 tsp turmeric
15 g/½ oz/1 tbsp flaked almonds
salt and freshly ground black pepper
fresh coriander, to garnish
cream, to garnish

1 Heat the oil in a frying pan and fry the minced beef and garlic for 5 minutes.

2 Add the cumin, coriander, garam masala and ginger. Cook for a further 2 minutes.

3 Add the ground almonds, season well and stir.

4 Pour in the coconut milk and stock. Mix well and bring to the boil.

5 Reduce the heat and simmer for about 20 minutes, stirring occasionally. Stir in the chopped fresh coriander.

6 Cook the rice in boiling salted water for 10-12 minutes or until al dente. Drain. Return to the pan and add the turmeric and flaked almonds. Serve with the curry and garnish with fresh coriander and a spoonful of cream.

COOK'S TIP
If coconut milk is unavailable, grate a block of creamed coconut into a bowL Pour on boiling water to dissolve, and strain into a jug.

Surf and Turf

Sometimes made with steak and lobster, this adaptation of an American theme, using minced beef and prawns, is equally delicious and much more economical.

Serves 4

For the minced beef patties
225 g/8 oz/2 cups minced beef
115 g/4 oz/2 cups fresh wholemeal
    breadcrumbs
4 spring onions, sliced
1 garlic clove, crushed
5 ml/1 tsp chilli powder
30 ml/2 tbsp oil
salt and freshly ground black pepper

For the sauce
25 g/1 oz/2 tbsp plain flour
150 ml/¼ pint/⅔ cup dry white wine
50 ml/2 fl oz/¼ cup vegetable stock
120 ml/4 fl oz/½ cup double cream
115 g/4 oz/½ cup tiger prawns

For the croûtes
24 slices white bread
25 g/1 oz/2 tbsp butter

2 Heat the oil and cook the patties for about 7 minutes, turning them frequently.

1 For the patties, mix the mince with the breadcrumbs, spring onions, garlic and chilli powder. Season and make four rounds.

3 For the sauce, add the flour to the frying pan and cook for I minute. Pour in the wine, stock, cream and prawns. Cook for 5 more minutes, stirring all the time.

4 For the croutes, stamp out four 10 cm/4 in bread rounds. Melt the butter and add the bread. Cook for 2-3 minutes, turning once. Remove and keep warm. Place the patties on the croûtes and top with sauce. Serve with mangetout.

Meatloaf

Another hugely popular dish all over the US, this tasty recipe is given an extra tangy taste with the addition of horseradish sauce, then served with a sour cream relish.

Serves 4

25 g/1 oz/2 tbsp butter
450 g/1 lb/4 cups minced beef
1 onion, chopped
2 garlic cloves, crushed
50 g/2 oz/½ cup bulgur wheat, soaked
25 g/2 oz/¼ cup freshly grated
  Parmesan cheese
1 celery stick, trimmed and sliced
30 ml/2 tbsp horseradish sauce
30 ml/2 tbsp tomato purée
25 g/1 oz/2 tbsp instant oatmeal
15 ml/1 tbsp chopped fresh thyme
fresh thyme, to garnish

For the relish
30 ml/2 tbsp horseradish sauce
150 ml/¼ pint/⅔ cup sour cream

1 Grease and line the base of a 675 g/ 1½ lb loaf tin. Preheat the oven to 180°C/350°F/Gas 4.

2 Melt the butter in a large pan and add the minced beef, onion and garlic. Cook for 7 minutes until browned and sealed.

3 Transfer the mixture to a bowl and add all of the remaining ingredients. Mix together well, season with salt and pepper and spoon into the prepared tin. Cover with foil.

4 Stand the loaf tin in a roasting tin and add I in/2.5 cm of water. Cook in the oven for 1½ hours. Mix the relish ingredients. Turn out the meatloaf and garnish with fresh thyme. Serve with fresh vegetables.

Moussaka

Originating in Greece, this simple, easy-to-make layered aubergine bake is well known worldwide and has become a popular dish in many homes and restaurants.

Serves 4

15 ml/1 tbsp oil
225 g/8 oz/2 cups minced lamb
5 ml/1 tsp ground cumin
1 red onion, chopped
25 g/8 oz/2 tbsp plain flour
175 ml/6 fl oz/¾ cup lamb stock
30 ml/2 tbsp tomato purée
15 ml/1 tbsp chopped fresh oregano
1 aubergine, sliced
salt and freshly ground black pepper

For the sauce
25 g/1 oz/2 tbsp butter
25 g/1 oz/2 tbsp plain flour
300 ml/½ pint/1¼ cup milk
50 g/2 oz/½ tbsp freshly grated
   Cheddar cheese
1 egg, beaten

1 Preheat the oven to 180°C/350°F/Gas 4. Heat the oil in a large pan and fry the lamb and cumin for 5 minutes

2 Add the onion and fry for a further 5 minutes, stirring occasionally.

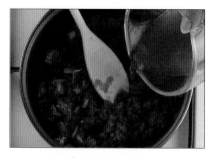

3 Add the flour and cook for I minute. Stir in the stock, tomato purée and fresh oregano. Bring to the boil. Reduce the heat and cook for 30 minutes.

4 Cover a plate with kitchen paper. Layer the sliced aubergine on top and sprinkle with salt. Stand for 10 minutes. Rinse thoroughly and pat dry.

5 For the sauce, melt the butter in a pan, add the flour and cook for I minute. Gradually stir in the milk and grated cheese, season well and bring to the boil, stirring continuously. Remove from the heat and stir in the egg.

6 Spoon the lamb into a dish, lay the aubergine on top and spoon on the sauce. Cook in the preheated oven for 45-60 minutes. Serve with a Greek salad.

VARIATION
If you wish, substitute the aubergine with potatoes. Thinly slice one large potato, parboil, drain and layer into the dish.

Greek Pasta Bake

This is an adaptation of a typical Greek dish, *Pastitsio*. This version is made with minced lamb and, instead of a white sauce, it is topped with creamy Greek yogurt before baking.

Serves 4

15 ml/l tbsp oil
450 g/l lb/4 cups minced lamb
1 onion, chopped
2 garlic cloves, crushed
30 ml/2 tbsp tomato purée
25 g/l oz/2 tbsp plain flour
300 ml/½ pint/1¼ cups lamb stock
2 large tomatoes
115 g/4 oz/1 cup pasta shapes
450 g/1 lb tub Greek yogurt
2 eggs
salt and freshly ground black pepper

3 Stir in the stock and season to taste. Bring to the boil and cook for 20 minutes.

4 Slice the tomatoes, place the meat in an ovenproof dish and arrange the tomatoes on top.

1 Preheat the oven to 190°C/375°F/ Gas 5. Heat the oil in a large pan and fry the lamb for 5 minutes. Add the onion and garlic and continue to fry for a further 5 minutes.

2 Stir in the tomato purée and flour. Cook for I minute.

5 Cook the pasta shapes in boiling salted water for 8-10 minutes or until *al dente*. Drain well.

6 Mix together the pasta, yogurt and eggs. Spoon on top of the tomatoes and cook in the preheated oven for I hour. Serve with a crisp salad.

VARIATION
Minced beef or pork would work equally well in this recipe. For an authentic Greek flavour, top the dish with Béchamel sauce and sprinkle with grated kefalotyri or halloumi cheese before baking.

Beef Ragout

A plate of couscous topped with a warmly spiced stew of minced beef with a selection of vegetables is reminiscent of the popular tagines of North Africa.

Serves 4

15 ml/l tbsp oil
450 g/l lb/4 cups minced beef
1 garlic clove, crushed
1 onion, quartered
25 g/l oz/2 tbsp plain flour
150 ml/¼ pint/⅔ cup dry white wine
150 ml/¼ pint/⅔ cup beef stock
2 baby turnips, chopped
115 g/4 oz swede, chopped
2 carrots, cut into chunks
2 courgettes, cut into chunks
15 ml/1 tbsp chopped fresh coriander
5 ml/1 tsp ground coriander
225 g/8 oz/2 cups couscous
salt and freshly ground black pepper
fresh coriander, to garnish

1 Heat the oil in a large pan. Add the minced beef and fry for 5 minutes. Add the garlic and onion. Cook for a further 3 minutes.

2 Stir in the flour and cook for about I minute. Add the wine and stock, season and bring to the boil, stirring all the time.

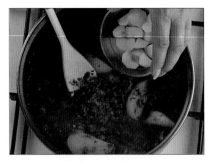

3 Add the vegetables and the fresh and ground coriander. Cover and simmer for 15 minutes. Put the couscous in a bowl, and cover with boiling water, for 10 minutes.

4 After 10 minutes drain and place in a lined steamer, and steam the couscous over the pan for a further 30 minutes. Garnish with fresh coriander and serve.

Beef Plait

This is an attractive alternative to a minced beef pie. The plaited pastry contains a flavourful filling and has a tasty baked cheese topping.

Serves 4

15 ml/1 tbsp oil
450 g/1 lb/4 cups minced beef
2 leeks, sliced
15 ml/1 tbsp tomato purée
15 ml/1 tbsp chopped fresh rosemary
25 g/1 oz/2 tbsp plain flour
150 ml/¼ pint/⅔ cup beef stock
450 g/1 lb prepared shortcrust pastry
25 g/1 oz/2 tbsp freshly grated
   Cheddar cheese
1 egg, beaten

1 Preheat the oven to 190°C/375°/Gas 5. Heat the oil in a large pan, add the minced beef and cook for 5 minutes. Stir in the leeks, tomato purée and fresh rosemary. Season well to taste.

2 Add the flour and cook for I minute. Stir in the stock gradually and cook for a further 20 minutes.

3 Roll out the prepared pastry onto a lightly floured surface to a large rectangle measuring about 30 x 25 cm/I2 x 10 in. Place the minced beef mixture in the centre of the pastry along the length.

4 Top with the grated cheese. Make parallel diagonal cuts either side of the filling, fold in each pastry end and then alternate pastry strips. Brush with beaten egg and cook for 40 minutes.

Chilli Beef Tortilla

Perhaps the best-known Mexican recipe (called *Chimichanga*), these wheat tortillas are filled with chilli beef, topped with a spicy cheese sauce and served with traditional accompaniments.

Serves 4

4 wheat tortillas

For the filling
15 ml/1 tbsp olive oil
450 g/l lb/4 cups minced beef
1 onion, chopped
5 ml/1 tsp paprika
1 red chilli, sliced
15 g/½ oz/1 tbsp plain flour
150 ml/¼ pint/⅔ cups beef stock
2 large tomatoes
salt and freshly ground black pepper
green peppers, chopped tomatoes, guacamole, sour cream, to serve

For the cheese sauce
25 g/1 oz/2 tbsp butter
25 g/1 oz/2 tbsp plain flour
300 ml/½ pint/1¼ cups milk
50 g/2 oz/½ cup Cheddar cheese, grated
pinch of paprika

1 Preheat the oven to 180°C/350°F/Gas 4. Heat the oil and fry the mince for 5 minutes. Add the onion, fry for 5 minutes.

2 Add the paprika, chilli and flour. Cook for I minute.

3 Stir in the stock. Season and bring to the boil. Simmer for 20 minutes.

4 For the cheese sauce, melt the butter in a large, heavy pan and add the flour. Cook for I minute and stir in the milk. Add the grated cheese and paprika, season to taste and bring to the boil, stirring continuously. Chop the tomatoes.

5 Place a little of the minced beef mixture along the length of each tortilla. Place the tomatoes on top, roll up into a 'cigar' shape and place seam-side down in an ovenproof dish.

6 Pour the cheese sauce over each tortilla and cook in the preheated oven for 20 minutes. Serve with green peppers, chopped tomato, guacamole and sour cream.

COOK'S TIP
Corn tortillas can be used instead of wheat, they are usually smaller and have a definite flavour of roasted corn.

Koftas

A simple but delicious way to serve spicy minced lamb. These tasty kebabs are quick to make and would be perfect for a light lunch or supper.

Serves 4

450 g/1 lb/4 cups minced lamb
75 g/3 oz/1½ cups fresh wholemeal
    breadcrumbs
1 onion, grated
5 ml/1 tbsp ground cumin
2 garlic cloves, crushed
1 egg, beaten
60 ml/2 fl oz/¼ cup lamb stock
salt and freshly ground black pepper

1 Place the minced lamb in a bowl and mash with a fork to form a paste.

2 Add the breadcrumbs and onion.

3 Stir in the cumin and garlic. Season.

4 Stir in the egg and stock with a fork. Using your hands bind the mixture together until smooth.

5 Shape into "sausages" with lightly floured hands.

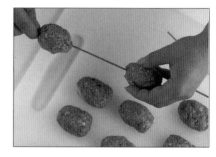

6 Thread onto wooden kebab skewers and grill under a medium heat for 30 minutes, turning occasionally. Serve with a crisp green salad and cucumber raita.

COOK'S TIP
Soak the wooden skewers in cold water for 30 minutes before using to prevent them from burning.

Sandwich Loaves

An interesting variation on a hot sandwich, these individual loaves are a nutritious, filling snack for lunch or supper, and they can be prepared in advance.

Serves 4

15 ml/1 tbsp oil
115 g/4 oz/1 cups minced beef
15 ml/1 tbsp horseradish sauce
15 ml/1 tbsp mustard
50 g/2 oz mangetout
1 leek, sliced
1 carrot, cut into strips
4 mini loaves
50 g/2 oz/¾ cup "no-need-to-soak"
    dried apricots, chopped
salt and freshly ground black pepper

1 Preheat the oven to 190°C/375°F/Gas 5. Heat the oil in a large pan and fry the minced beef for around 5 minutes until brown and sealed. Add the horseradish sauce and mustard and season well to taste.

COOK'S TIP
Reserve the bread from the centre of the loaves and make it into breadcrumbs. Freeze for future recipes such as stuffing and burgers.

2 Place the vegetables and apricots in a pan of lightly salted boiling water. Cook for 5 minutes and drain.

3 Slice the tops from the loaves and reserve them. Scoop out the centre of the loaves, leaving a 1.25 cm/½ in shell.

4 Layer the beef, vegetables and apricots into the loaves, packing the ingredients down well. Replace the lid, wrap in foil and cook for 35 minutes in the preheated oven. Serve sliced.

Stuffed Tomatoes

This easy and quick recipe demonstrates the versatility of mince as a stuffing, when combined with tasty bulgur wheat, crunchy celery and cashew nuts.

Serves 4

4 beef tomatoes
7.5 ml/½ tbsp oil
75 g/3 oz/¾ cup minced beef
1 small red onion, thinly sliced
25 g/1 oz/¼ cup bulgur wheat
30 ml/2 tbsp freshly grated
    Parmesan cheese
15 g/½ oz/1 tbsp unsalted cashew
    nuts, chopped
1 small celery stick, chopped
salt and freshly ground black pepper

1 Trim the top from the tomatoes, scoop out the flesh with a teaspoon and reserve. Blanch the tomatoes for 2 minutes in boiling water and drain well.

2 Heat the oil in a large pan, add the minced beef and onion, and cook for 10 minutes. Stir in the tomato flesh. Place the bulgur wheat in a bowl, cover with boiling water and leave to soak for 10 minutes. Drain if necessary.

3 Mix the mince and bulgur, grated cheese, nuts and celery. Season well.

4 Spoon the filling into the tomatoes and grill under a medium heat for 10 minutes. Serve with a crisp green salad.

Pancake Parcels

Making good use of the different types of mince, these quick and easy pancakes are filled with a delicious turkey and apple mixture, and served with cranberry sauce.

Serves 4

For the filling
30 ml/2 tbsp oil
450 g/l lb/4 cups minced turkey
30 ml/2 tsp chopped fresh chives
2 green eating apples, cored and diced
25 g/l oz/2 tbsp flour
175 ml/6 fl oz/¾ cup chicken stock
salt and freshly ground black pepper

For the pancakes
115 g/4 oz/1 cup plain flour
pinch of salt
1 egg, beaten
300 ml/½ pint/1¼ cups milk
oil for frying

For the sauce
60 ml/4 tbsp cranberry sauce
60 ml/2 fl oz/¼ cup chicken stock
15 ml/1 tbsp clear honey
15 g/ ½ oz/1 tbsp cornflour

1 For the filling, heat the oil and fry the turkey for 5 minutes. Add the chives and apples then the flour.

2 Stir in the stock and seasoning. Cook for 20 minutes. For the pancakes, sift the flour into a bowl with a pinch of salt. Drop the egg in the centre, beating it with the milk to form a smooth batter.

3 Heat the oil in a l5 cm/6 in omelette pan. Pour off the oil and add one-quarter of the pancake mixture. Tilt the pan to spread the mixture and cook for 2-3 minutes. Turn the pancake and cook for a further 2 minutes. Keep warm.

4 For the sauce, heat the cranberry sauce, stock and honey until melted. Blend the cornflour with 20 ml/4 tsp water, stir it in and bring to the boil, stirring until clear.

5 Lay the pancakes on a chopping board, spoon the filling into the centre and fold over around the filling. Place each pancake on a plate and spoon on some of the sauce. Serve with a fresh vegetable such as mangetout.

Speedy Pizzas

Always popular as a snack, this flavourful pizza will also please the cook as it is so quick to make. It uses ready-baked muffins as a filling base.

Serves 4

2 muffins

For the topping
10 ml/2 tsp oil
115 g/4 oz/1 cup minced beef
1 small onion, sliced
15 g/½ oz/1 tbsp plain flour
50 ml/2 fl oz/¼ cup beef stock
15 ml/1 tbsp tomato purée
½ green pepper, seeded and chopped
6 pitted black olives, sliced
25 g/1 oz mozzarella cheese, sliced
salt and freshly ground black pepper

For the sauce
25 g/1 oz/2 tbsp butter
25 g/1 oz/2 tbsp plain flour
150 ml/¼ pint/1⅔ cups milk
30 ml/2 tbsp chopped fresh basil

1 Preheat the oven to 200°C/400°F/ Gas 6. Heat the oil, add the mince and onion and cook for 8 minutes. Add the flour, stock, tomato purée and pepper. Season and cook gently for 7 minutes.

2 For the sauce, melt the butter in a pan, add the flour and cook for I minute. Gradually stir in the milk and bring to the boil, add the basil and season to taste.

3 Cut each muffin in half and spoon a little sauce onto each one.

4 Top each muffin half with some of the mince mixture, olives and mozzarella cheese. Cook in the oven for 10-15 minutes until the cheese has melted, then serve with coleslaw and a crisp green salad.

Rissoles

Minced beef is blended with potato and herbs then coated and fried and served with a tasty dip, to provide an economical and satisfying light meal or appetizer.

Serves 4

450 g/1 lb potatoes, cubed
175 g/6 oz/1½ cups minced beef
3 spring onions, chopped
15 ml/1 tbsp chopped fresh parsley
1 egg, beaten
115 g/4 oz/1 cup dried wholemeal
    breadcrumbs
oil for deep-frying
salt and freshly ground black pepper

For the dip
120 ml/4 fl oz/½ cup mayonnaise
120 ml/4 fl oz/½ cup natural yogurt
15 ml/l tbsp chopped fresh parsley

1 Cook the potatoes in a pan of lightly salted boiling water for 20 minutes. Drain.

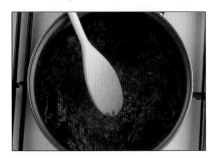

2 Dry-fry the minced beef in a large pan for 5 minutes. Add the spring onions and cook for a further 2 minutes.

COOK'S TIP
Minced raw or cooked lamb can be used to make the rissoles, and rosemary or mint could be added instead of parsley.

3 Stir in the fresh parsley and season well to taste.

4 Mash the potatoes and mix into the mince. Roll into eight sausage-shaped rissoles with lightly floured hands.

5 Place the egg in a shallow dish and the breadcrumbs in another. Dip the rissoles into the egg to coat them and then roll in the crumbs to cover each one completely.

6 Heat the oil in a large heavy-based pan for deep-frying to 170°C/350°F. Cook the rissoles in two batches for 5-7 minutes or until golden. Drain well. Mix the dip ingredients together and serve with cherry tomatoes and lambs lettuce.

Fritters

Coated in batter and lightly fried, this tasty alternative to beef patties need only be served with a light salad to provide a substantial snack.

Serves 4

For the patties
225 g/8 oz/2 cups minced beef
1 onion, grated
10 ml/2 tsp chopped fresh oregano
50 g/2 oz/½ cup canned
    sweetcorn, drained
5 ml/1 tbsp mustard
115 g/4 oz/2 cups fresh white
    breadcrumbs
oil for deep-frying
salt and freshly ground black pepper

For the batter
115 g/4 oz/1 cup plain flour
60 ml/2 fl oz/¼ cup warm water
40 g/1½ oz/3 tbsp melted butter
60 ml/2 fl oz/¼ cup cold water
1 egg white

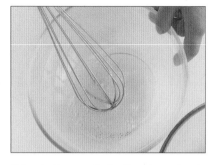

3 For the batter, sift the flour into a bowl and stir in the warm water and melted butter. Mix to a smooth batter with the cold water. Whisk the egg white until peaking and fold into the mixture.

4 Heat the oil for deep-frying to 160°C/325°F. Dip the patties into the batter to coat and fry two at a time in the oil. Drain on absorbent kitchen paper and serve with tomato pickle and green salad.

1 For the patties, place the minced beef in a bowl and mash with a fork. Add the onion, oregano, sweetcorn, mustard and breadcrumbs. Season well.

2 Form into eight round patties.

Nachos

The addition of minced beef to this traditional starter demonstrates the use of mince as an excellent extender, creating a filling, quick meal.

Serves 4

225 g/8 oz/2 cups minced beef
2 red chillies, chopped
3 spring onions, chopped
175 g/6 oz nachos
300 ml/½ pint/1¼ cups soured cream
50 g/2 oz/½ cup freshly grated
    Cheddar cheese
salt and freshly ground black pepper

1 Dry-fry the minced beef and chillies in a large pan for 10 minutes, stirring all the time.

2 Add the spring onions, season and cook for a further 5 minutes.

3 Arrange the nachos in four individual flameproof dishes.

4 Spoon on the mince mixture, top with soured cream and grated cheese, then grill under a medium heat for 5 minutes.

Beef Pasties

These meat and vegetable filled parcels may be made in advance and frozen. With their filling of minced beef and root vegetables, they are perfect for cool autumn days.

2 Add the flour and cook for I minute. Stir in the stock and season to taste. Cook over a gentle heat for 10 minutes. Stir in the fresh parsley and cool.

3 Roll out the pastry to a large rectangle. Cut eight I5 cm/6 in circles.

4 Spoon the filling onto one half of each pastry circle, brush the edges with egg and fold in half to form a semi-circle Crimp the edges and roll. Brush the pasties with egg and place on a baking sheet. Cook for 35 minutes or until golden. Serve with a crisp salad.

Serves 8

15 ml/1 tbsp oil
175 g/6 oz/1½ cups minced beef
15 ml/1 tbsp tomato purée
1 onion, chopped
1 carrot, diced
50 g/2 oz turnip, diced
1 large potato, diced
25 g/1 oz/2 tbsp plain flour
150 ml/¼ pint/⅔ cup beef stock
15 ml/1 tbsp chopped fresh parsley
450 g/1 lb prepared shortcrust pastry
1 egg, beaten
salt and freshly ground black pepper

1 Preheat the oven to 190°C/375°F/Gas 5. Heat the oil in a large pan and add the minced beef. Cook for 5 minutes. Stir in the tomato purée, onion, carrot turnip and potato. Cook for a further 5 minutes.

Soufflé Omelette

Requiring a small degree of skill, this light omelette should be prepared and served immediately to fully appreciate its texture and flavour.

Serves 4

For the filling
15 ml/1 tbsp oil
225 g/8 oz/2 cups minced beef
1 onion, quartered
40 g/1½ oz/3 tbsp plain flour
150 ml/¼ pint/⅔ cup red wine
150 ml/¼ pint/⅔ cup beef stock
3 bacon rashers, de-rinded and chopped
5 ml/1 tsp paprika
50 g/2 oz/½ cup freshly grated
    Gruyére cheese
salt and freshly ground black pepper

For the omelette
8 eggs, separated
120 ml/4 fl oz/½ cup water
25 g/1 oz/2 tbsp butter

1 For the filling, heat the oil in a large pan. Add the minced beef and cook for 5 minutes. Stir in the onion and cook for a further 5 minutes. Add the flour and pour in the red wine, stock and bacon. Season to taste and add the paprika. Cook over a low heat while preparing the omelette.

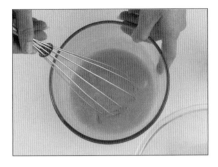

2 For the omelette, whisk the egg yolks until creamy. Season to taste and pour in the water and whisk again. Whisk the egg whites until peaking.

3 Melt one-quarter of the butter in a 15 cm/6 in omelette pan. Fold the egg whites into the yolk mixture and pour one-quarter of the mixture into the pan. Cook for 2-3 minutes until golden-brown on the underside.

4 Grill under a medium heat for 2-3 minutes or until browned. Loosen with a spatula and spoon in one-quarter of the grated cheese and one-quarter of the mince filling. Fold over the omelette and serve immediately. Repeat with the remaining filling and omelette mixture. Serve with freshly cooked vegetables.

Stilton Burger

Slightly more up-market than the traditional burger, this tasty recipe contains a delicious surprise. Stilton cheese is encased in a crunchy burger to make a mouthwatering, melting filling.

Serves 4

450 g/1 lb/4 cups minced beef
1 onion, finely chopped
1 celery stick, chopped
5 ml/1 tsp dried mixed herbs
5 ml/1 tsp prepared mustard
50 g/2 oz/½ cup crumbled Stilton cheese
4 burger buns
salt and freshly ground black pepper

1 Place the minced beef in a bowl together with the onion and celery. Season well.

2 Stir in the herbs and mustard, bringing them together to form a firm mixture.

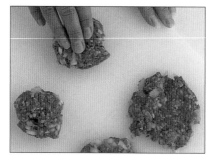

3 Divide the mixture into eight equal portions. Place four on a chopping board and flatten each one slightly.

4 Place the crumbled cheese in the centre of each.

5 Flatten the remaining mixture and place on top. Mould the mixture together encasing the crumbled cheese and shape into four burgers.

6 Grill under a medium heat for 10 minutes, turning once or until cooked through. Split the burger buns and place a burger inside each. Serve with salad and mustard pickle.

COOK'S TIP

For a more substantial meal, serve with roasted potato wedges and sautéed onions and mushrooms.

Peasant Bolognese

A spicy version of a popular family dish, this minced beef sauce is enlivened with the rich flavours of Worcestershire sauce and chorizo sausages.

Serves 4

15 ml/l tbsp oil
225 g/8 oz/2 cups minced beef
1 onion, chopped
5 ml/1 tsp ground chilli powder
15 ml/1 tbsp Worcestershire sauce
25 g/1 oz/2 tbsp plain flour
150 ml/¼ pint/⅔ cup beefstock
4 chorizo sausages
50 g/2 oz baby sweetcorn
1 x 200 g/7 oz can chopped tomatoes
15 ml/1 tbsp chopped fresh basil
salt and freshly ground black pepper

1 Heat the oil and fry the minced beef for 5 minutes. Add the onion and chilli powder and cook for a further 3 minutes.

2 Stir in the Worcestershire sauce and flour. Cook for I minute before pouring in the stock.

3 Slice the chorizo sausages and halve the corn lengthways.

4 Stir in the sausages, tomatoes, sweetcorn and chopped basil. Season well and bring to the boil. Reduce the heat and simmer for 30 minutes. Serve with spaghetti, garnished with fresh basil.

COOK'S TIP
Make up the Bolognese sauce and freeze in conveniently sized portions for up to 2 months.

Spicy Beef Stir-Fry

Promoting a fast-growing trend in worldwide cuisine, the wok is used in this recipe to produce a deliciously healthy stir-fry, with minced beef and crunchy vegetables.

Serves 4

15 ml/1 tbsp oil
450 g/1 lb/4 cups minced beef
2.5 cm/1 in fresh root ginger, sliced
5 ml/1 tsp five-spice powder
1 red chilli, sliced
50 g/2 oz mangetout
1 red pepper, seeded and chopped
1 carrot, sliced
115 g/4 oz beansprouts
15 ml/1 tbsp sesame oil

1 Heat the oil in a wok until very hot. Add the mince and cook for 3 minutes, stirring.

2 Add the ginger, five-spice powder and chilli. Cook for I minute.

3 Add the mangetout, pepper and carrot and cook for a further 3 minutes, stirring continuously.

4 Add the beansprouts and sesame oil and cook for another 2 minutes. Serve immediately with noodles.

Pork Crumble

Minced pork combines with the sweetness of apple and the texture of crunchy vegetables. With a crispy cheese and oat topping, this is a meal to tempt all the family.

Serves 4

For the filling
15 ml/1 tbsp oil
450 g/1 lb/4 cups minced pork
1 onion, sliced
25 g/1 oz/2 tbsp plain flour
150 ml/¼ pint/⅔ cup milk
150 ml/¼ pint/⅔ cup vegetable stock
50 g/2 oz broccoli florets
50 g/4 oz/½ cup canned
    sweetcorn, drained
1 green eating apple, cored and diced
salt and freshly ground black pepper

Ingredients
50 g/2 oz/½ cup instant oatmeal
50 g/2 oz/½ cup plain flour
15 g/½ oz/1 tbsp butter
25 g/2 oz/¼ cup freshly grated Red
    Leicester cheese

1 Preheat the oven to 180°C/350°F/Gas 4. For the filling, heat the oil in a large pan and fry the pork for 5 minutes. Add the onion and continue to fry for a further 3 minutes.

2 Stir in the flour and cook for 1 minute. Pour in the milk and stock and bring to the boil, stirring all the time.

3 Add the broccoli, sweetcorn and apple.

4 Spoon the mixture into four individual ovenproof dishes.

5 For the crumble topping, mix the oatmeal and flour, then rub in the butter.

6 Spoon the topping onto the pork mixture and press down with the back of a spoon. Scatter over the cheese and place in the pre-heated oven. Cook for 45 minutes. Garnish with apple and serve.

VARIATION
For a rich cheesy topping, mix crushed potato crisps and grated cheese. Cook as before.

Risotto

An Italian dish made with short grain arborio rice which gives a creamy consistency to this easy one-pan recipe. Chicken, green beans, peppers and chestnut mushrooms add flavour and texture.

Serves 4

15 ml/1 tbsp oil
175 g/3 oz/1½ cups arborio rice
1 onion, chopped
225 g/8 oz/2 cups minced chicken
600 ml/1 pint/2½ cups chicken stock
1 red pepper, seeded and chopped
1 yellow pepper, seeded and chopped
75 g/3 oz frozen green beans
115 g/4 oz chestnut mushrooms, sliced
15 ml/1 tbsp chopped fresh parsley
salt and freshly ground black pepper
fresh parsley, to garnish

1 Heat the oil in a large frying pan. Add the rice and cook for 2 minutes until transparent.

2 Add the onion and minced chicken. Cook for 5 minutes, stirring occasionally.

3 Pour in the stock and bring to the boil.

4 Add the peppers and simmer 10 minutes.

5 Add the green beans and mushrooms, mix thoroughly, and cook for a further 10 minutes, stirring.

6 Stir in the fresh parsley and season well to taste. Cook for 10 minutes or until the liquid has been absorbed. Serve, garnished with fresh parsley.

COOK'S TIP
Look out for other varieties of risotto rice. Carnaroli is resistant to overcooking and produces a creamy risotto. Vialone nano has a high starch content and also makes a very creamy risotto, while baldo is the quickest risotto rice to cook.

Stuffed Cabbage

This traditional English dish steps into the realm of fusion food with its Middle Eastern-style filling of spiced minced beef, sultanas and chickpeas.

Serves 4

1 savoy cabbage
15 ml/1 tbsp oil
115 g/4 oz/1 cup minced beef
1 red onion, chopped
15 ml/1 tbsp chopped fresh thyme
25 g/1 oz/2 tbsp plain flour
25 g/1 oz/¼ cup sultanas
150 ml/¼ pint/⅔ cup beef stock
50 g/2 oz/½ cup canned
    chickpeas, drained
5 ml/1 tsp garam masala
50 g/1 oz/1 cup fresh wholemeal
    breadcrumbs
salt and freshly ground black pepper

1 Preheat the oven to 200°C/400°F/ Gas 6. Remove the outer leaves from the cabbage. Blanch the remaining cabbage in boiling water for 5 minutes. Drain well.

2 Heat the oil in a large pan and fry the minced beef for 5 minutes. Add the onion and the thyme and cook for a further 3 minutes.

3 Stir in the flour and cook for 1 minute. Add the sultanas and slowly pour in the stock, stirring all the time.

4 Stir in the chickpeas and garam masala. Remove the mixture from the heat and add the breadcrumbs. Mix and season well with salt and pepper.

5 Trim the top from the cabbage and scoop out the centre.

6 Spoon in the mince mixture, wrap in foil and bake in the preheated oven for 30 minutes. Serve with freshly cooked vegetables such as potatoes and carrots.

COOK'S TIP
Use the filling to stuff beefsteak tomatoes, cooked aubergines or peppers. Grill under a medium heat for 10-15 minutes.

VARIATION
In place of the chickpeas, use whichever canned beans you have available; red kidney beans or navy beans would work well in this recipe.

Cannelloni

This Italian dish has quickly become popular, offering many variations to the original recipe. This version introduces a variety of vegetables which are topped with a traditional cheese sauce.

Serves 4

8 cannelloni tubes
115 g/4 oz spinach

For the filling
15 ml/1 tbsp oil
175 g/6 oz/1½ cups minced beef
2 garlic cloves, crushed
25 g/1 oz/2 tbsp plain flour
120 ml/4 fl oz/½ cup beefstock
1 small carrot, finely chopped
1 small yellow courgette, chopped
salt and freshly ground black pepper

For the sauce
25 g/1 oz/2 tbsp butter
25 g/1 oz/2 tbsp plain flour
250 ml/8 fl oz/1 cup milk
50 g/2 oz/½ cup freshly grated
    Parmesan cheese

1 Preheat the oven to 180°C/350°F/Gas 4. For the filling, heat the oil in a large pan. Add the minced beef and garlic. Cook for about 5 minutes.

2 Add the flour and cook for a further 1 minute. Slowly stir in the stock and bring to the boil.

3 Add the carrot and courgette, season well and cook for 10 minutes.

4 Spoon the mince mixture into the cannelloni tubes and place in an ovenproof dish.

COOK'S TIP
In this versatile recipe you can substitute minced chicken for beef and include all the family's favourite vegetables. Try celery, mushrooms and a mixture of red, yellow and green peppers.

5 Blanch the spinach in boiling water for 3 minutes. Drain well and place on top of the cannelloni tubes.

6 For the sauce melt the butter in a pan. Add the flour and cook for 1 minute. Pour in the milk, add the grated cheese and season well. Bring to the boil, stirring all the time. Pour over the cannelloni and spinach and cook for 30 minutes in the preheated oven. Serve with tomatoes and a crisp green salad.

Chicken Bouche

A spectacular centrepiece, this light pastry case contains a delicious chicken and mushroom filling with a hint of fruit. Ideal served with freshly cooked vegetables.

Serves 4

450 g/1 lb prepared puff pastry
beaten egg

For the filling
15 ml/1 tbsp oil
450 g/1 1b/4 cups minced chicken
25 g/1oz/2 tbsp plain flour
150 ml/¼ pint/⅔ cup milk
150 ml/¼ pint/⅔ cup chicken stock
4 spring onions, chopped
25 g/1 oz/¼ cup redcurrants
75 g/3 oz button mushrooms, sliced
15 ml/1 tbsp chopped fresh tarragon
salt and freshly ground black pepper

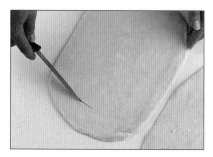

1 Preheat the oven to 200°C/400°F/Gas 6. Roll half the pastry out on a lightly floured work surface to a 25 cm/10 in oval. Roll out the remainder to an oval of the same size and draw a smaller 20 cm/ 8 in oval in the centre.

2 Brush the edge of the first pastry shape with the beaten egg and place the smaller oval on top. Place on a dampened baking sheet and cook for 30 minutes in the preheated oven.

3 For the filling, heat the oil in a large pan. Fry the minced chicken for 5 minutes. Add the flour and cook for a further I minute. Stir in the milk and stock and bring to the boil.

4 Add the spring onions, redcurrants and mushrooms. Cook for 20 minutes.

5 Stir in the fresh tarragon and season the mixture to taste.

6 Place the pastry bouche on a serving plate, remove the oval centre and spoon in the filling. Place the oval lid on top. Serve with freshly cooked vegetables.

VARIATION
You can also use shortcrust pastry for this dish and cook as a traditional chicken pie.

Pasta Timbales

An alternative way to serve pasta for a special occasion. Mixed with minced beef and tomato and baked in a lettuce parcel, it makes an impressive dish for a dinner party.

Serves 4

8 cos lettuce leaves

For the filling
15 ml/1 tbsp oil
175 g/6 oz/1½ cups minced beef
15 ml/1 tbsp tomato purée
1 garlic clove, crushed
115 g/4 oz/¾ cup macaroni
salt and freshly ground black pepper

For the sauce
25 g/1 oz/2 tbsp butter
25 g/1 oz/2 tbsp plain flour
250 ml/8 fl oz/1 cup double cream
30 ml/2 tbsp chopped fresh basil

1 Preheat the oven to 180°C/350°F/Gas 4. For the filling, heat the oil in a large pan and fry the minced beef for about 7 minutes until it begins to brown. Add the tomato purée and garlic and cook for 5 minutes.

2 Cook the macaroni in boiling water for 8-10 minutes or until *al dente*. Drain.

3 Mix together the pasta and mince.

4 Line four 150 ml/¼ pint/⅔ cup ramekin dishes with the cos lettuce leaves. Season the mince and spoon into the lettuce-lined ramekins.

5 Fold the lettuce leaves over the mince mixture and place in a roasting tin half-filled with boiling water. Cover and cook for 20 minutes.

6 For the sauce melt the butter in a pan. Add the flour and cook for 1 minute. Stir in the cream and fresh basil. Season and bring to the boil, stirring all the time. Turn out the timbales and serve with the basil sauce.

COOK'S TIP
A crisp green salad of leaves and herbs would perfectly complement this pasta dish.

Fish Bites with Crispy Cabbage

An oriental element is added to these attractive and tasty fish bites. Coated in sesame seeds and served with traditional deep-fried cabbage, they are sure to impress.

Serves 8

For the fish bites
350 g/12 oz/1½ cups peeled prawns
350 g/12 oz cod fillets
10 ml/2 tsp light soy sauce
10 ml/2 tsp sesame seeds
oil for deep-frying

For the cabbage
225 g/8 oz savoy cabbage
pinch of salt
15 g/½ oz/1 tbsp flaked almonds
spring roll sauce, to serve

1 Put the prawns and cod in a food processor and blend for 20 seconds. Place in a bowl and stir in the soy sauce.

2 Roll the mixture into sixteen balls and toss in the sesame seeds to coat.

3 Heat the oil for deep-frying to 160°C/325°F. Shred the cabbage and place in the hot oil. Fry for 2 minutes. Drain well and keep warm. Lightly sprinkle the cabbage with salt and toss in the almonds.

4 Fry the balls in two batches for about 5 minutes until golden-brown. Remove with a draining spoon. Serve with the cabbage, and spring roll sauce for dipping.

Mince Wellington

Making use of a popular recipe, this variation retains all the flavours of the original, but an expensive fillet of beef is replaced with a savoury minced beef filling.

Serves 4

For the filling
15 ml/1 tbsp oil
900 g/2 lb/8 cups minced beef
1 red onion, chopped
2 garlic cloves, crushed
25 g/1 oz/2 tbsp plain flour
150 ml/¼ pint/⅔ cup red wine
30 ml/2 tbsp chopped fresh oregano
75 g/3 oz/¾ cup wild and long grain rice
1 egg, beaten
salt and freshly ground black pepper

For the pastry case
450 g/1 lb prepared puff pastry
225 g/8 oz Ardennes pâté
50 g/2 oz/½ cup mixed chopped nuts
beaten egg to glaze

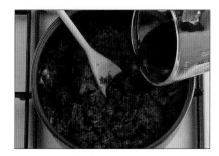

1 Preheat the oven to 200°C/400°F/Gas 6. For the filling, heat the oil in a pan. Add the minced beef, onion and garlic, and fry for 10 minutes. Stir in the flour and cook for a further I minute. Stir in the wine and bring to the boil. Add the oregano and cook for 20 minutes.

2 Cook the rice in boiling salted water for 10 minutes or until *al dente*. Drain well and stir into the mince mixture with the egg. Season to taste and cool.

3 Roll out the pastry to a 35 X 25 cm/14 x 10 in rectangle. Trim the edges and reserve. Place the mince mixture in the centre of the pastry along its length. Top with the pâté and nuts.

4 Brush the edges of the pastry with egg and fold around to encase the filling. Turn over and arrange the pastry trimmings in a lattice pattern on top. Brush with the beaten egg and place on a dampened baking sheet. Cook in the preheated oven for 45 minutes. Serve with freshly cooked vegetables.

Filo Pie

Ready-made filo pastry is easy to use and very effective in appearance. Thin sheets of folded pastry encase a lightly spiced, fruity lamb filling to make a tasty and attractive pie.

Serves 4

15 ml/l tbsp oil
450 g/1 lb/4 cups minced lamb
1 red onion, sliced
30 ml/2 tbsp chopped fresh coriander
25 g/1 oz/2 tbsp plain flour
300 ml/½ pint/1¼ cups lamb stock
50 g/1 oz/½ cup canned
    chickpeas, drained
5 ml/l tsp ground cumin
225 g/8 oz filo pastry
115 g/4 oz/1¼ cups "no-need-to-soak"
    dried apricots
1 courgette, sliced
25 g/1 oz/2 tbsp melted butter
salt and freshly ground black pepper

1 Preheat the oven to 190°C/375°F/Gas 5. Heat the oil in a large pan. Add the minced lamb and cook for 5 minutes. Stir in the onion, fresh coriander and flour and cook for a further 1 minute.

2 Pour in the lamb stock and chickpeas. Season to taste and stir in the cumin. Cook for 20 minutes.

3 Line a deep ovenproof dish with four sheets of filo pastry.

4 Spoon in the mince mixture. with dried apricots and courgette.

5 Lay two sheets of filo pastry on top of the filling and brush with the melted butter. Fold the remaining sheets on top. Pour on the remainder of the butter and cook in the oven for 40 minutes. Serve with freshly cooked vegetables.

COOK'S TIP
Filo pastry dries out quickly and cracks easily, so always cover it with baking parchment or a clean tea towel, then a damp tea towel, to keep it flexible.

Chicken Roule

A relatively simple dish to prepare, this recipe use mince as a filling. It is rolled in chicken meat which is spread with a creamy garlic cheese that just melts in the mouth.

Serves 4

4 boneless chicken breasts, about
    115 g/4 oz each
115 g/4 oz/1 cup minced beef
30 ml/2 tbsp chopped fresh chives
225 g/8 oz garlic-flavoured cream cheese
30 ml/2 tbsp clear honey
salt and freshly ground black pepper

1 Preheat the oven to 190°C/375°F/Gas 5. Place the chicken between sheets of clear film. Beat with a meat mallet until it is 6 mm/¼ in thick and joined together.

2 Fry the minced beef for 3 minutes then add the fresh chives and seasoning. Cool.

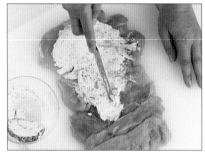

3 Place the chicken on a board and spread with the cream cheese, leaving a narrow margin all around.

4 Spread the minced beef mixture over the roule.

5 Carefully roll up the chicken from the narrow end, to form a sausage shape.

6 Brush with honey and place in a roasting tin. Cook for 1 hour in the preheated oven. Remove from the tin and slice thinly. Serve the roule with freshly cooked vegetables.

COOK'S TIP
Garlic-flavoured cream cheese is made from cow's milk. It is usually bought in a log shape, and when sliced, the layer of added seasoning appears as a spiral. It comes in other flavours, including chives, salmon and herb.

Chow Mein

One of the most well-known authentic Chinese dishes, this recipe is basically noodles fried with meat and vegetables, seasoned with soy sauce, ginger and sesame oil.

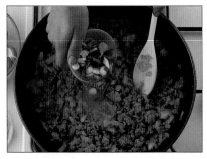

3 Stir in the Chinese five-spice powder. Add the pork and cook for 10 minutes, stirring continuously. Add the spring onions, mushrooms, bamboo shoots and continue to cook for a further 5 minutes.

4 Stir in the noodles and sesame oil. Mix all the ingredients together well and serve with prawn crackers.

COOK'S TIP

You can use fresh egg noodles for this dish. Blanch them in hot water to soften them and to remove some of the starch. Take care to drain off excess water before they are stir-fried.

Serves 4

225 g/8 oz dried egg noodles
30 ml/2 tbsp oil
1 onion, chopped
1.25 cm/½ in fresh root ginger, chopped
2 garlic cloves, crushed
30 ml/2 tbsp soy sauce
60 ml/2 fl oz/¼ cup dry white wine
10 ml/2 tsp Chinese five-spice powder
450 g/1 lb/4 cups minced pork
4 spring onions, sliced
50 g/2 oz oyster mushrooms
75 g/3 oz bamboo shoots
15 ml/1 tbsp sesame oil
prawn crackers, to serve

1 Cook the noodles in boiling water for 4 minutes and drain.

2 Meanwhile, heat the oil in a wok and add the onion, ginger, garlic. soy sauce and wine. Cook for 1 minute.

Beef Stroganoff

A great standby when entertaining, beef Stroganoff is a very easy dish to prepare. Simply serve with rice, pasta or noodles for a quick and very tasty meal.

Serves 4

15 ml/1 tbsp oil
450 g/1 oz/4 cups minced beef
1 onion, quartered
30 ml/2 tbsp tomato purée
25 g/1 oz/2 tbsp plain flour
450 ml/³⁄₄ pint/2 cups beefstock
1 green pepper, seeded, halved and sliced
115 g/4 oz open cap mushrooms, sliced
300 ml/¹⁄₂ pint/1¹⁄₄ cups sour cream
salt and freshly ground black pepper
fresh parsley, to garnish

3 Add the green pepper and mushrooms. Cook for a further 20 minutes.

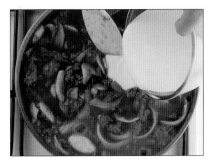

4 Stir in half of the soured cream and cook for 10 minutes. Garnish with fresh parsley and serve with freshly cooked rice and the remaining sour cream.

1 Heat the oil in a frying pan. Add the minced beef and cook for 5 minutes. Stir in the onion, tomato purée and flour. Cook for 1 minute.

2 Stir in the beef stock. Season well and bring to the boil.

COOK'S TIP
Beef stroganoff is traditionally served with pasta but it is also good with rice or mashed potatoes. It is quite rich, so serve with green beans, broccoli or a salad.

Cheeseburgers

Homemade burger are popular with all the family. This version is made with bulgur wheat, onion and parsley and served in a lightly toasted bun with favourite fries on the side.

Serves 4

50 g/2 oz/½ cup bulgur wheat
225 g/2 oz/2 cups minced beef
1 onion, sliced
15 ml/1 tbsp chopped fresh parsley
15 ml/1 tbsp tomato purée
15 ml/1 tbsp freshly grated
    Parmesan cheese
1 egg beaten
4 burger buns
lettuce leaves
4 cheese slices
tomato relish
salt and freshly ground black pepper

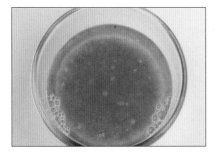

1 Place the bulgur wheat in a bowl and add enough boiling water to cover. Leave to stand for 10 minutes. Drain off any excess liquid if necessary.

COOK'S TIP
Let the kids assemble their own burgers; provide them with alternative relishes and pickles for added interest!

2 Put the minced beef into a bowl and break up with a fork.

3 Place the onion and fresh parsley in a food processor and process for 20 seconds. Add to the beef.

4 Stir in the tomato purée and grated cheese. Season well. Add the drained bulgur wheat.

5 Stir in the beaten egg and bring the mixture together. Shape into four burgers with your hands. Grill for 8-10 minutes each side under a medium heat or until cooked through.

6 Split the burger buns in half and place a burger inside each one with some lettuce leaves. Top with a cheese slice and a spoonful of relish and the burger bun top. Serve with fries and a crisp green salad.

Calzone

A tasty minced beef and spinach filling in a tangy cheese sauce is encased in a simple dough to make a folded pizza that is easy to eat while on the move.

Serves 4

For the dough
450 g/1 lb/4½ cups self-raising flour
115 g/4 oz/½ cup butter
250 ml/8 fl oz/1 cup milk

For the filling
15 ml/l tbsp oil
175 g/6 oz/1½ cups minced beef
15 ml/l tbsp chopped fresh basil
1 onion, sliced
25 g/1 oz/2 tbsp plain flour
150 ml/¼ pint/⅔ cup beef stock
115 g/4 oz spinach, shredded
beaten egg to glaze

For the sauce
15 g/½ oz/1 tbsp oil butter
15 g/½ oz/1 tbsp plain flour
150 ml/¼ pint/⅔ cup milk
60 ml/2 fl oz/¼ cup grated Parmesan
5 ml/1 tsp mustard

1 Preheat the oven to 200°C/425°F/Gas 7. Sift the flour. Rub in the butter until the mixture resembles breadcrumbs.

2 Stir in the milk and bring the mixture together to form a dough. Cut into four equal pieces and roll each one into a 15 cm/6 in circle.

3 For the filling, heat the oil in a large pan, add the mince and cook for 5 minutes. Stir in the basil and onion. Season and add the flour. Cook for I minute. Stir in the stock and bring to the boil. Cook for 10 minutes.

4 Blanch the spinach for 2 minutes and drain. Place the dough circles on an oiled baking sheet and spoon spinach on one half of each circle. Top with the mince.

5 For the sauce, melt the butter and add the flour. Cook for I minute. Stir in the milk, cheese and mustard and bring to the boil, stirring all the time.

6 Spoon the sauce onto the mince and spinach. Dampen the edges of the dough with water and fold over to encase the filling and form semi-circles. Brush with beaten egg and cook for 20 minutes. Serve with a crisp green salad.

COOK'S TIP
Like pasties and turnovers, calzone pizzas are perfect for picnics or whenever you are on the move.

Stuffed Naan

Naan breads are a popular alternative to burger buns. Mini naans are warmed and split and filled with a minced meat patty. For an authentic touch, serve with mango chutney and salad.

Serves 4

15 g/4 oz/1 cup minced beef
115 g/4 oz/1 cup pork sausagemeat
5 ml/1 tsp mixed dried herbs
15 ml/1 tbsp brown sauce
4 mini naan breads
60 ml/4 tbsp mango chutney
salt and freshly ground black pepper

1 Place the minced beef in a bowl and break up with a fork.

2 Add the sausagemeat and herbs and season well. Stir in the brown sauce.

3 Bring the mixture together with your hands and form into four patties. Grill under a medium heat for 8 minutes, turning once.

4 Place the naan breads under a medium grill for 2-3 minutes. Split with a knife and place the patties and chutney inside. Serve with a crisp green salad.

COOK'S TIP

Minced chicken would work well in this recipe. Use a chicken tikka sauce instead of the brown sauce, and add some chopped fresh coriander in place of the mixed dried herbs.

Bean Bake

This is a variation on a hot-pot. A tasty mixture of minced beef, baked beans and a tangy barbecue sauce is topped with slices of potato for a filling nutritious meal for winter evenings.

Serves 4

2 large potatoes, sliced
15 ml/1 tbsp oil
350 g/12 oz/3 cups minced beef
1 onion, sliced
300 g/10 oz can baked beans
90 ml/6 tbsp barbecue sauce
50 g/2 oz/½ cup freshly grated
    Gruyere cheese
salt and freshly ground black pepper
chopped fresh parsley, to garnish

1 Preheat the oven to 200°C/400°F/Gas 6. Cook the potatoes in boiling water for 10 minutes. Drain well and reserve.

2 Heat the oil in a large pan and fry the minced beef and onion for 5 minutes.

VARIATION
If you wish, substitute the baked beans with any canned beans of your choice and replace the barbecue sauce with tomato ketchup.

3 Add the baked beans and barbecue sauce. Season well. Spoon into the base of an ovenproof dish.

4 Arrange the sliced potatoes so they overlap on top of the mince. Sprinkle with the cheese and cook for 30 minutes in the preheated oven. Remove from the oven, sprinkle with the fresh parsley and serve with freshly cooked vegetables.

Beef Pie

This is a fun-packed meal specially for the kids. It is a version of shepherd's pie, with a pastry topping instead of potato. A face with cress hair will help to encourage a child to eat a meal.

Serves 4

15 ml/1 tbsp oil
175 g/6 oz/1½ cups minced beef
115 g/2 oz large beef sausages
25 g/1 oz/2 tbsp plain flour
1 x 200 g/7 oz can chopped tomatoes
90 ml/6 tbsp beef stock
30 ml/2 tbsp chopped fresh parsley
60 ml/2 fl oz/¼ cup cup tomato ketchup
15 ml/1 tbsp granulated sugar
300 g/11 oz prepared shortcrust pastry
beaten egg to glaze
salad cress, to garnish

2 Slice the sausages and add to the pan. Cook for a further 5 minutes. Add the flour and cook for I minute.

4 Roll out half of the pastry onto a lightly floured surface to line a round pie dish. Spoon in the filling and trim the edges. Brush with egg.

5 Roll out the remaining pastry for the lid. Cut out two 'eyes' and a 'mouth' and place on top of the pie. Knock up the edges and seal. Brush the pastry with beaten egg, and cook for 30 minutes in the preheated oven.

1 Preheat the oven to 190°C/375°F/Gas 5. Heat the oil in a large pan and fry the minced beef for 5 minutes.

3 Stir in the chopped tomatoes, stock, fresh parsley, ketchup and sugar. Cook for 10 minutes, stirring occasionally.

VARIATION
This mixture can also be used as the filling for a cottage pie for adults. Just top with mashed potato, sprinkle with grated cheese and cook as before.

6 Remove the pie from the oven and arrange the cress around the top of the pie for the 'hair', Serve immediately with freshly cooked vegetables.

Popovers

Universally popular, these individual Yorkshire puddings made from sweetcorn batter are filled with tasty meatballs then baked and served with vegetables or baked beans.

Serves 4

For the batter
150 g/2 oz/½ cup plain flour
pinch of salt
1 egg
150 ml/¼ pint/⅔ cup milk
50 g/2 oz/½ cup canned
    sweetcorn, drained
15 g/2 oz/1 tbsp butter

For the filling
115 g/4 oz/1 cup minced beef
1 red onion, chopped
30 ml/2 tbsp tomato relish
50 g/2 oz/1 cup fresh wholemeal
    breadcrumbs
15 ml/1 tbsp oil
salt and freshly ground black pepper

1 Preheat the oven to 220°C/425°F/Gas 7. For the batter sift the flour and salt into a bowl. Make a well in the centre.

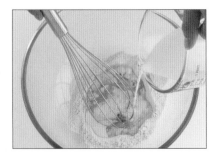

2 Crack the egg and whisk into the flour mixture, add the milk gradually to form a smooth batter. Add the sweetcorn.

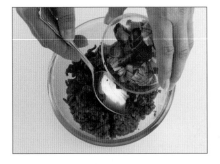

3 For the filling, place the minced beef in a bowl. Add the onion and seasoning.

4 Stir in the tomato relish and breadcrumbs and bring the mixture together. Roll into four equal-sized balls.

5 Heat the oil in a large pan and fry the mince balls to seal. Place the butter in a four-section Yorkshire pudding tin. Put into the preheated oven until melted.

6 Divide the batter between each section of the tin and place a meatball in the centre of each. Cook for 30 minutes. Remove from the oven and serve with freshly cooked vegetables or a salad.

COOK'S TIP
The key to making great popovers is having the eggs and milk at room temperature or warm before mixing. Popovers do not freeze well

Ham and Egg Pots

It is easy to mince any meat to produce quick and economical meals. Here cooked ham is finely minced and cooked in individual dishes with spinach, pineapple and egg for a nutritious meal.

Serves 4

175 g/6 oz/1½ cups cooked ham
5 ml/1 tsp dried thyme
30 ml/2 tbsp Worcestershire sauce
50 g/2 oz spinach, shredded
50 g/2 oz/½ cup crushed canned
    pineapple in natural juice, drained
4 eggs
salt and freshly ground black pepper

COOK'S TIP
Serve ham and egg pots with toast or pitta fingers for a more substantial lunch for a child, and for more flavour, use smoked cooked ham.

2 Blanch the spinach in boiling water for 2 minutes. Drain well.

3 Spoon alternate layers of ham, spinach and pineapple into four 150 ml/¼ pint/⅔ cup ramekin dishes.

4 Top each pot with an egg. Cover with buttered foil and place in a roasting tin half-filled with water. Cook for 20 minutes. Serve with a green salad.

1 Preheat the oven to 200°C/400°F/Gas 6. Place the ham in a food processor for 30 seconds to mince. Transfer to a bowl and season. Stir in the thyme and Worcestershire sauce.

Chilli Con Carne

An American recipe that has become a regular feature in many homes. Simple and economical, it is one of the most popular minced beef recipes developed.

Serves 4

15 ml/1 tbsp oil
225 g/8 oz/2 cups minced beef
1 onion, quartered
5 ml/1 tsp chilli powder
15 g/1 oz/2 tbsp plain flour
30 ml/2 tbsp tomato purée
150 ml/¼ pint/⅔ cup beefstock
1 x 100 g/7 oz can chopped tomatoes
1 x 200 g/7 oz can kidney beans, drained
1 green pepper, seeded and chopped
15 ml/1 tbsp Worcestershire sauce
75 g/3 oz/½ cup long grain rice
salt and freshly ground black pepper
sour cream, to serve
fresh parsley, to garnish

3 Add the kidney beans, green pepper and Worcestershire sauce. Reduce the heat, simmer and continue to cook for 45 minutes.

4 Meanwhile cook the rice in boiling salted water for 10-12 minutes. Drain. Spoon on to the serving plate. Add the chilli with a spoonful of sour cream, and garnish with fresh parsley.

1 Heat the oil in a large pan and fry the minced beef, onion and chilli powder for 7 minutes.

2 Add the flour and tomato purée and cook for I minute. Stir in the stock and tomatoes and bring to the boil.

Beef Dough Balls

A great way to use up any leftover pizza dough, dough balls are easy to make and contain a delicious cheesy meatball in the centre.

Serves 4

For the dough
225 g/8 oz/2 cups self-raising flour
50 g/2 oz/4 tbsp butter
120 ml/4 fl oz/½ cup milk
beaten egg to glaze

For the filling
175 g/6 oz/1½ cups minced beef
15 ml/1 tbsp tomato purée
25 g/1 oz/¼ cup frozen peas
25 g/1 oz/¼ cup freshly grated
    mozzarella cheese
salt and freshly ground black pepper

1 Preheat the oven to 200°C/400°F/
Gas 6. For the dough, sift the flour into a bowl. Rub in the butter until the mixture resembles breadcrumbs. Gradually stir in the milk to form a dough.

2 Cut the dough into sixteen equal pieces and roll into 10 cm/4 in circles on a lightly floured surface.

3 For the filling, dry-fry the minced beef for 3 minutes, stirring all the time. Add the tomato purée and peas.

4 Remove the pan from the heat and stir in the grated cheese. Season well.

5 Spoon the mixture into the centre of each dough circle. Dampen the edges of the dough and bring to the centre, folding around to encase the mince mixture. Pinch together at the top.

6 Carefully re-shape into balls and place on an oiled baking sheet. Cook in the preheated oven for 20 minutes. Serve with a crunchy salad.

Index